631ART.COM PRESENTS:
"BIRDS OF PREY"
BY EDDIE ALFARO
I0837698

BIRDS OF PREY HAVE
EXCELLENT EYESIGHT.

OSPREY

HAWKS ARE THE MOST KEEN-EYED AND EFFICIENT HUNTERS.

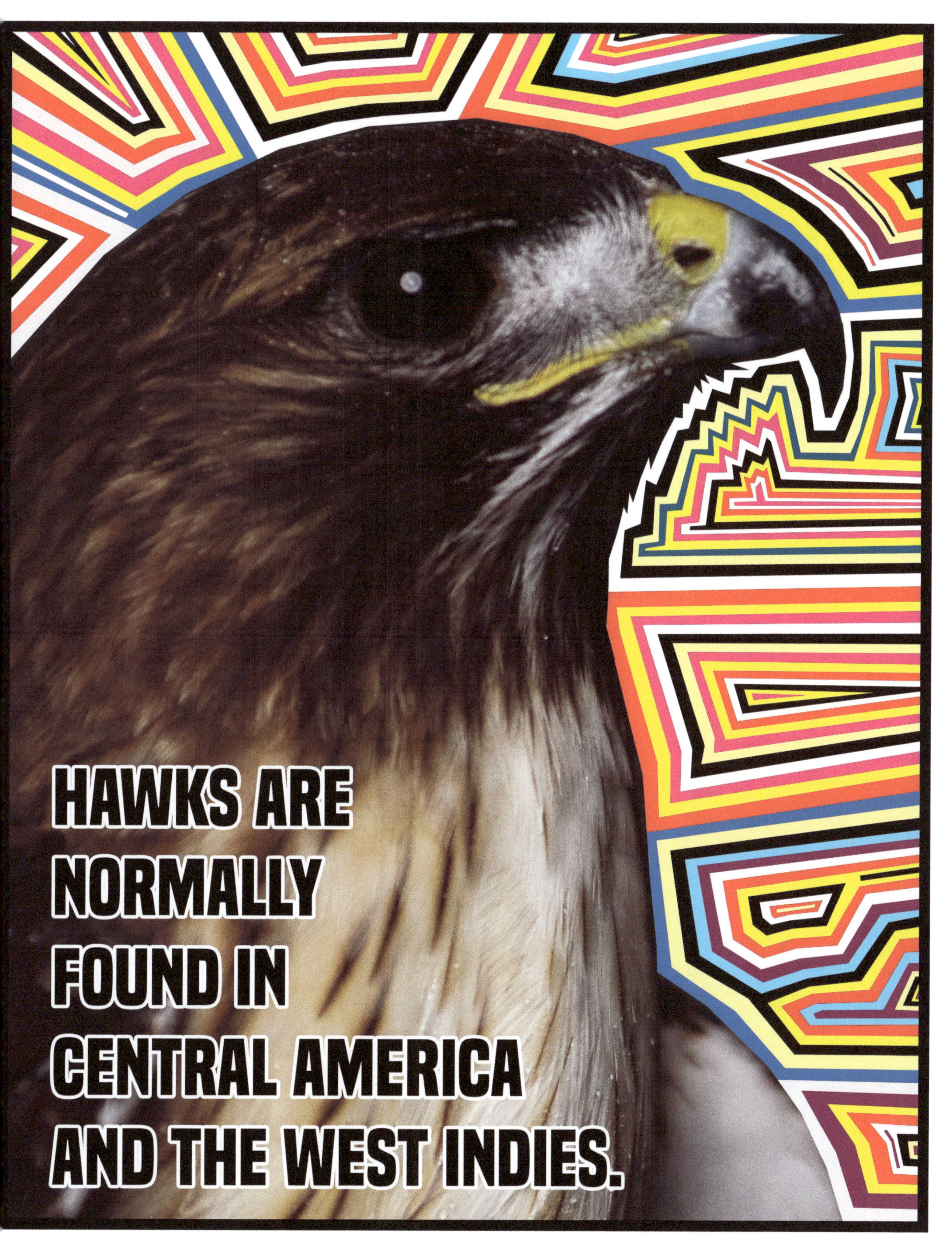

HAWKS ARE
NORMALLY
FOUND IN
CENTRAL AMERICA
AND THE WEST INDIES.

MANY BIRDS OF PREY CAN DO
TRICKS AND FLIPS IN THE AIR.

WHITE TAILED EAGLE

KITE

BIRD OF PREY ARE ANY BIRD THAT
PURSUES OTHER ANIMALS FOR FOOD.

OSPREYS AND OWLS MATE FOR LIFE. THEY ARE GOOD PARENTS.

THE CALIFORNIA CONDOR IS THE LARGEST LAND BIRD IN NORTH AMERICA.

A HAWK CAN FLY AT SPEEDS WHICH
MAY REACH UP TO 150 MILES PER
HOUR WHILE DIVING DOWN!

RAPTOR

VULTURE

THERE ARE AROUND 200 DIFFERENT OWL SPECIES.

CARACARA

MOST OWLS HUNT INSECTS, SMALL MAMMALS AND OTHER BIRDS.

THE BALD EAGLE HAS BEEN THE NATIONAL EMBLEM OF THE UNITED STATES SINCE 1782.

INTERESTING FACTS ABOUT BIRDS OF PREY:

AN EAGLE'S EYESIGHT IS AROUND 5 TIMES BETTER THAN THE HUMAN'S VISION.

HUMANS HAVE USED FALCONS FOR HUNTING FOR THOUSANDS OF YEARS.

AN OWL'S EYES ACCOUNT FOR 1-5% PERCENT OF THE OWL'S BODY WEIGHT.

EAGLE BEAKS BEND WITH AGE.

AN OWL HAS THE BEST NIGHT VISION OF ANY ANIMAL.

FALCONS CAN PROCESS FOUR TYPES OF LIGHT WHILE HUMANS CAN ONLY PROCESS THREE.

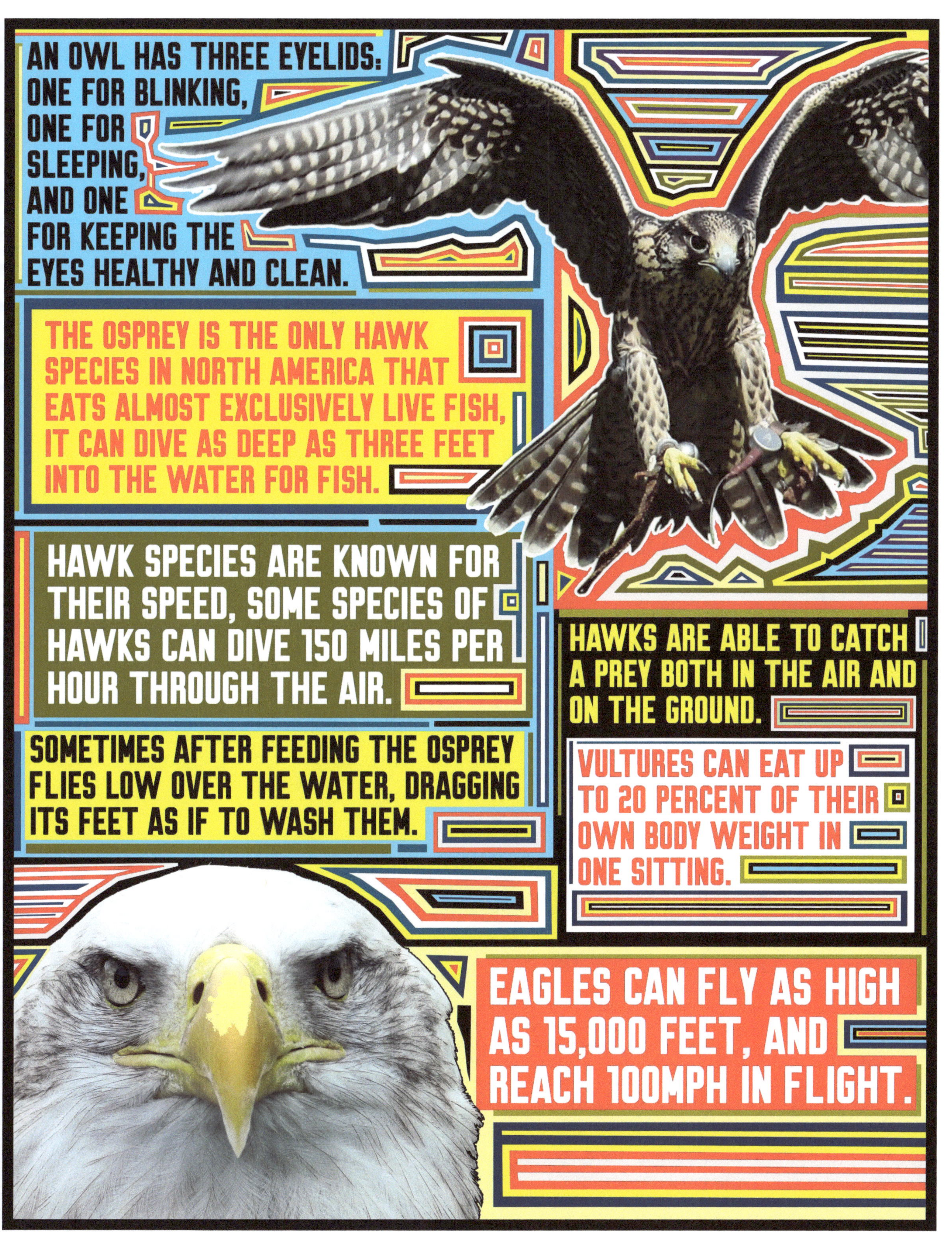

AN OWL HAS THREE EYELIDS: ONE FOR BLINKING, ONE FOR SLEEPING, AND ONE FOR KEEPING THE EYES HEALTHY AND CLEAN.
THE OSPREY IS THE ONLY HAWK SPECIES IN NORTH AMERICA THAT EATS ALMOST EXCLUSIVELY LIVE FISH, IT CAN DIVE AS DEEP AS THREE FEET INTO THE WATER FOR FISH.
HAWK SPECIES ARE KNOWN FOR THEIR SPEED, SOME SPECIES OF HAWKS CAN DIVE 150 MILES PER HOUR THROUGH THE AIR.
SOMETIMES AFTER FEEDING THE OSPREY FLIES LOW OVER THE WATER, DRAGGING ITS FEET AS IF TO WASH THEM.
HAWKS ARE ABLE TO CATCH A PREY BOTH IN THE AIR AND ON THE GROUND.
VULTURES CAN EAT UP TO 20 PERCENT OF THEIR OWN BODY WEIGHT IN ONE SITTING.
EAGLES CAN FLY AS HIGH AS 15,000 FEET, AND REACH 100MPH IN FLIGHT.

THANK YOU.
THE END.

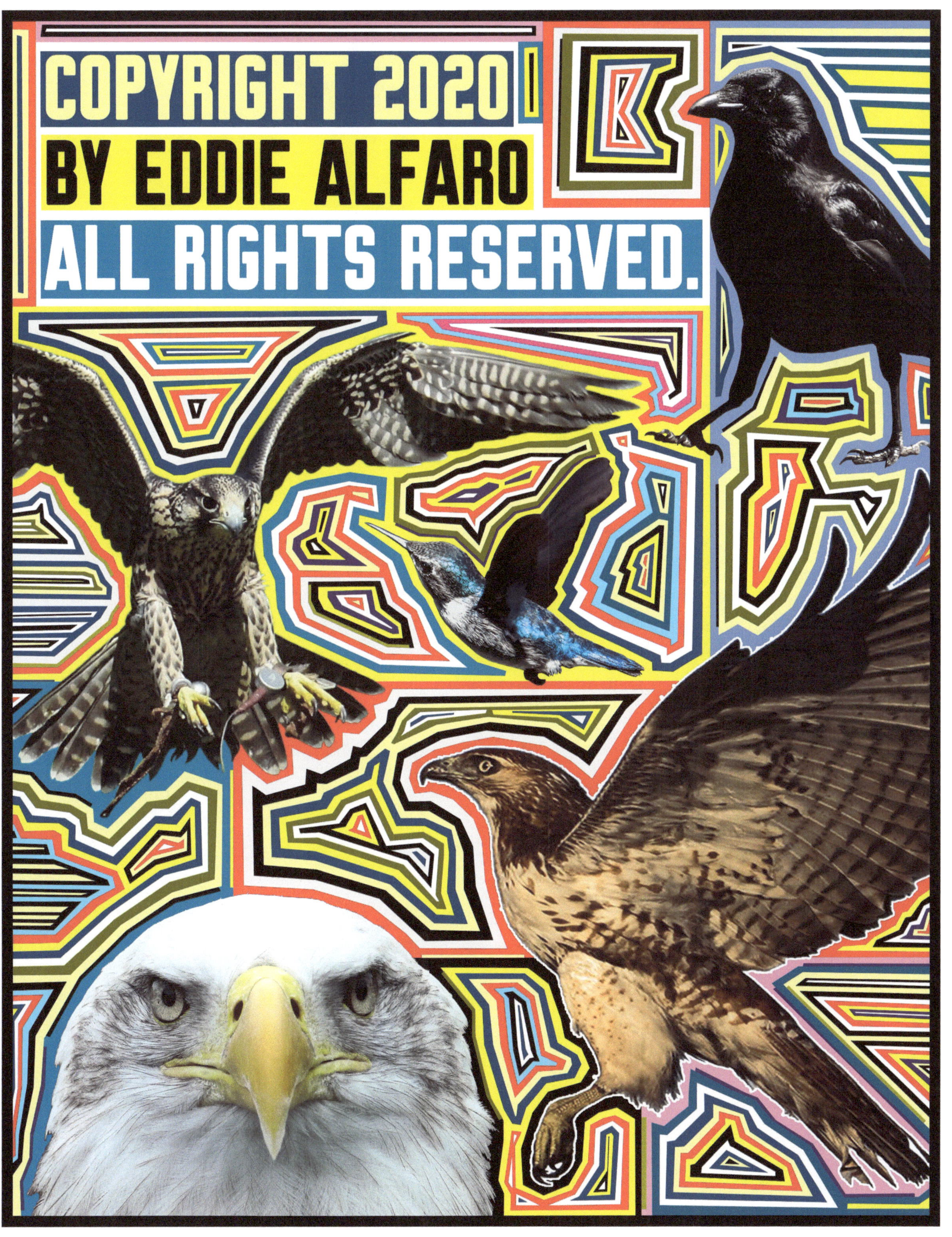
COPYRIGHT 2020
BY EDDIE ALFARO
ALL RIGHTS RESERVED.

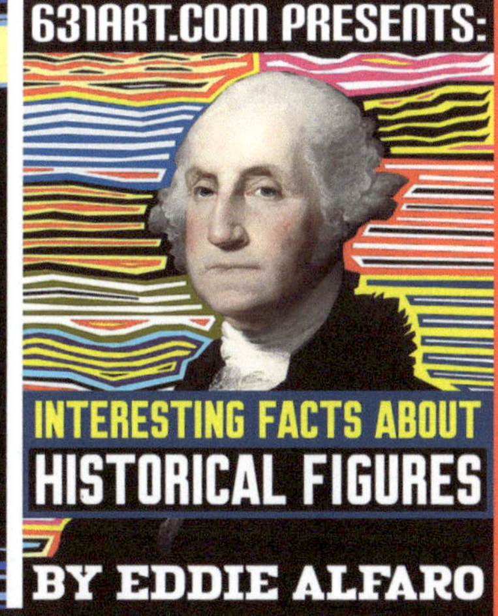

MORE BOOKS AT:

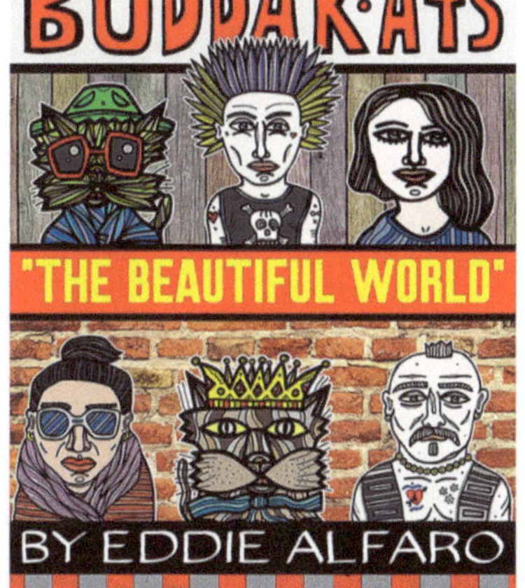

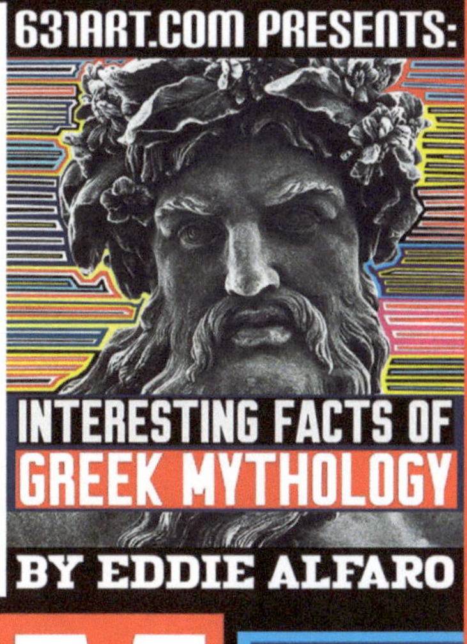

631ART.COM

www.ingramcontent.com/pod-product-compliance
Lightning Source LLC
Chambersburg PA
CBHW040137240726
48664CB00002B/513